# More praise for *Truth and Other Lies*

In this poignant collection, Pris Campbell tells us the story of how she fell in love, waited for him while he trained as a naval officer at OCS, got married in the romantically magical land of Hawaii, and then divorced all the while the Vietnam War was ripping the soul of America in two. Campbell masterfully casts a spell over us as she relives their past and how the present is haunted by the hopes and dreams of her first marriage. History, particularly the events on the fringes and margins of a horrific war, walks side by side with their fated romance, told by an exemplary humane narrator."— **Michael Parker**, author of *Divining the Spirits in the House of the Hush and Hush.*

Grief takes on many faces, shifts hot and cold, changes through the omnivorous jaws of time. In Pris Campbell's most recent book, *Truth and Other Lies*, we learn how a war can consume not only its soldiers, but also those who loved them. Her vivid and honest poems put architecture to the thinning walls of angst and PTSD. In full color, set in the trauma of the 1960's anti-war movement, we find a collection of poems that draws us toward empathy and compassion, finding in "Fourteen Months," an uncommon truth: "He's dead two years and a half now... poems spill out like the turning tide he rode on then and ride again now, touching me occasionally within our shared Vietnam of the soul." This is narrative poetry at a visceral level, provocative, naked, and essential.
— **Edward Nudelman**, author of *Thin Places.*

# Truth and Other Lies

PRIS CAMPBELL

Nixes Mate Books
Allston, Massachusetts

Copyright © 2022 Pris Campbell

Book design by d'Entremont
Cover photograph used with permission.

All rights reserved. This book or any portion thereof may not be reproduced or used in any manner whatsoever without the express written permission of the publisher except for the use of brief quotations in a book review or scholarly journal.

ISBN 978-1-949279-40-5

Nixes Mate Books
POBox 1179
Allston, MA 02134
nixesmate.pub

*This hill is won. That hill is lost.*

*Dedicated to Vietnam Veterans and their families.*

# Contents

| | |
|---|---|
| So it Began | 3 |
| Drafted | 5 |
| Upside Down | 7 |
| Around the World | 9 |
| Letters | 12 |
| Storm | 13 |
| Safe | 15 |
| White Beside White | 16 |
| Rearrangements | 17 |
| Deja vu | 18 |
| (Tanka) | 19 |
| Changeling | 20 |
| West Wind Rerun | 22 |
| (Tanka) | 23 |
| Apologies | 24 |
| Disappearance | 25 |
| (Tanka) | 27 |
| Moving On | 28 |
| Newport Blues | 29 |
| Amnesia | 31 |

| | |
|---|---:|
| Forgotten Places | 33 |
| Measure of Time | 34 |
| Parting | 36 |
| Blood On the Wall | 37 |
| Doing Time | 39 |
| Truth and Other Lies | 41 |
| Cocoon | 42 |
| Who Sleeps With Him Now | 43 |
| Old bones | 44 |
| My First Ex | 45 |
| Battlefield | 47 |
| Bed of Nails | 49 |
| Untouched | 51 |
| Over | 53 |
| Fourteen Months | 54 |
| Contemplating My Mortality | 56 |
| Time's Tales | 58 |
| For a Moment | 60 |
| Flutter | 61 |
| Acknowledgments | 64 |
| About the author | 65 |

Truth and Other Lies

## So it Began

An unwanted blind date
with a man just handed a low draft number
in these crazy Vietnam years.
My friend only wanted this chance to get
together with his best friend
who dumped her, pregnant, and unhelped
in these days of illegal abortions.

I plan to make my excuses early,
leave my matchmaking friend,
the pizza, the restaurant
and come back, away from
this man I was pushed to meet.
It's my last summer of grad school
and I can claim my dissertation needs me.

Big brown eyes under curly hair.
A shy smile.
The question, 'are you Pris'?

A voice inside of me,
some strange knowing,
perhaps my childhood fairy godmother, says.
'this is the man you will marry'.

How silly. He's a stranger,
a man I know nothing about,
but I don't make my excuses early.
I eat the pizza and we can't stop talking.

We talk that night and more nights to come.
'God bless Karen' we say of my friend,
neither of us religiously inclined.

# Drafted

He can run off
to Canada, go to jail,
or disappear into the jungles
of Vietnam, perhaps never
to be seen again so he signs up for OCS.
Unless he's assigned to a Navy river boat,
the odds of us ending up together
after this dirty war could improve.

We make the most of our summer
before he leaves and I head off for
the job I already signed a contract
for in Missouri.

Already the forces of war pull us apart.

Sgt Pepper's lonely hearts club band
Is out and he buys the album.
We turn out the lights in his apartment,

let the music, this new sound, wash
over us, forgetting the war, forgetting
we will soon part, forgetting he still
may not come back.

# Upside Down

Every time we turn on the radio,
"A Whiter Shade of Pale" is dispersed
between body counts of the Viet Cong
showing we're winning.

One is as crazy as the other
but the strange song seems to fit the times
and becomes 'our' song' by default.

Every day, the news…
This hill is won.
That hill is lost.

G.I's march in with ears
on their belts.
GI's burn villages to kill hidden Cong,
desperate powder kegs posing as men
run loose to avenge broken bodies
of friends.

Heads of Cong sit on stakes
until they are stopped
adding to the horror
that should be a surreal movie.
Unpopular officers are fragged.
Pot becomes a cottage industry.

We hear the stories from the disenchanted
war torn, slandered men returning,
hearts in their hands,
minds still over there in the jungles
with their dead buddies.

I hold his hand tight
each time 'our' song plays.
Yes, in this craziness, we've
decided to marry on his other
side of it.

Something to come home to.
Something to hope for.

## Around the World

He's at OCS and my grad school friends
have scattered as if a stiff wind
had blown them all away.
One good friend a year ahead of me
works where I am and becomes
my life line to sanity since I hate this job
I had expected to like.

My time has been indentured
to the clock maker.
Work fills my days and evenings.
Lessons to plan. Tests to grade
when all of my time at work out of class
is filled with counseling students.
Like a continuation of the slavery
of grad school, which I loved
but was ready to escape.

In December my bipolar never-came
out-of-the-closet gay friend and co-worker
kills himself. No warning.
Just a note and he's gone.

Calling OCS is forbidden so letters fly.
I inherit my friend's counseling students
along with my teaching and become so
overwhelmed with work and buried
in student grief and my own
until I fall down Alice's hole.

My fairy godmother didn't warn me
about this part.

A new friend and co-worker fishes me out
and helps me walk the days on remote control.
I write OCS daily but what can
he say except that he loves me and warns
that his mail can be read. I ignore news

of the war. We still don't know if he'll be
assigned to a ship or river boat.

In the spring I'm ensured of a job
in Hawaii when my contract ends in the fall.
I can wait for him there.

"A Whiter Shade of Pale" comes on the radio
for the first time since summer
and I'm with him again in my heart.

## Letters

His love letters arrive from Vietnam,
not one by one like teardrops,
but in bundles, like heavy rainfall,
and so I race home from work
breathlessly to see if today
is Christmas yet.

I add new letters to the other letters
to read and reread, the only part
of him I can touch, his body
committed to the war whore.

# Storm

When I feel lonely
despite Hawaii's beauty
surrounding me
as I wait, work,

I imagine him
on the other side
of a thick wall.
I can't see him,
can't hear him,
but I know he's there.
I've been a year now
by that wall.
In his parsed out letters,
he imagines holding me,
making babies,
me as the perfect wife.
He writes about shipmates,
trips to the Philippines

for fuel and repairs,
storms they push through at sea.
He rarely mentions Vietnam,
the far larger storm there.

## Safe

Crepe paper flowers surround us,
Navy wives chattering with excitement.
The ship, due any day!
Our job?
The biggest lei Hawaii has seen,
for a tug to hoist high to bow
when the ship returns to port.
I slip one pale flower onto the link, think,
'just now – this very second – one more has died'.
Finally, the ship steams into Pearl,
bearing that colorful lei.
Sailors in white, scattered formations
salute from tiered decks,
navy band blaring 'stars and stripes'.
He's back at last,
back to where only where our dreams
could bring us these past 14 months.

## White Beside White

We walk white beside white
under the sword arch
into the searing Hawaii sun,
past rice-tossing friends,
the rising scent of gardenias,
the waving palm trees,
into our new life.

This moment sears itself
into my memory banks
to relive whenever storms appear.

# Rearrangements

We move from my studio apartment
to a two bedroom high above Waikiki.
He comes bearing gifts from the ship's R&R
in Hong Kong – dishes, silverware with carved,
wooden handles, a camera, fire opal earrings.

For our marriage, he tells me.

He's leaner and tan, a bit more withdrawn
than when I last saw him, but still is the same man.
We walk the beach to the sound of ukes,
weave leis for our necks, party with our Navy friends.
Hawaii has felt like home from my first step
off the plane.

We pretend the four months
will drag by before the ship's next tour
into hell.

## Deja vu

I see us in my mind's eye again waiting
as the ship docks.

My heart flutters.
My stomach does the rumba.

I don't yet know the toll being in Vietnam
has taken but I will find out.

I will lose the dream.

But that's all in my future.
At our wedding reception,
I dance.

# (Tanka)

the scents of Hawaii
drift into our bedroom
thoughts of Nam
lurk as we make love, knowing
the hourglass is draining

# Changeling

A Sunday.
Nowhere we want to go.
We read, listen to Bloomfield.

Suddenly the world upends.
He grows wings, flaps
around our tiny apartment
in these lush Hawaii hills.

I follow, but he
shoves me away.
'I feel trapped', he says,
this frightening feathered creature
who no longer resembled the man
who carved out his rib,
gave it to me for safekeeping,
who just shared my bed,
whispering words of love.

He races outside, attempting
a getaway from his prison, built
finally into explosive overload
with the byproducts of war.

When he returns two hours later,
he tells me he decided to stay with me
because he promised…no words of love,
I reinsert the rib, hoping his talons will retract,
that feathers will molt, but he jerks away.
My palms split open.

## West Wind Rerun

In my dreams, I still glide,
in that mist of white,
under the arch of swords slicing
the Hawaiian sky.

Beside me, finally, this man...
back in his Navy dress whites
back from the haze of Napalm and Orange,
the smiling bar girls
back to this day, this new wife,
whore-goddess of his love letters,
co-pilot for re-entry.

I didn't know then of the scars
criss-crossing his heart,
or that his blood would burst hot
through its seams, burning my dress,
staining my ring, melting my flesh
or that a west wind was already rising
to clatter my bones away.

(Tanka)

bundled letters
to remember him by...
one last strained kiss
before the ship disappears
back into war's stench

## Apologies

Letter after letter arrive saying
he's sorry, that he loved me
'underneath' the whole time.

Promises are made that
things will be different
but can I believe the ice
around my heart can thaw
so easily, that promises made
when he's out of my space
will hold true when he re-enters.

I want to believe that our love words
over our summer, in our letters
can't be tossed this easily, war or not.

# Disappearance

He returns from his second tour
but I can smell that war,
despite his vows of love.
It seeps from his bones.

We were so certain
before Vietnam.
Of us.
Our lives together,
the babies he wanted
to make.

When the shells
hit his ship during this tour he fell
deeper into his hole.

He doesn't want me
to drop braids, kiss a frog,
or click heels together
to bring him back.

I watch helplessly
as he continues his tumble,
reach out, but my hands
touch empty space.

## (Tanka)

tour over
in this palm-filled paradise
aloha oe…
slowly steamed lau lau's
laced with sadness

## Moving On

Land duty.
Newport.
Home to the America's Cup,
the Bermuda Race,
the wealthy in their mansions
by the sea.

We eat clam chowder
at the Black Pearl, wander
the docks in these days
before the Cup is taken,
the docks transformed
into a shopping mall.

He continues his drift.
In a boat he would be halfway
across the sea.

I pretend to be happy,
hope that pretend will become real.

# Newport Blues

Sailors wander the streets of Newport,
hats cocked to one side
and a Gene Kelly spring in their stride.
War isn't yet a teacher,
wiping their innocence clean.

My cousin came back from the 'big one',
just to be killed on the road by a drunk
with far better aim than the Germans.

With my husband land-based in Newport,
I scour the cobblestone streets
for some sign my cousin had been there.
Maybe I thought ghosts of old sailors
returned to where their free fall began,
came to retrace their path home.
Back to their mother's arms.
Back to a lover's embrace.
No different, really, in that longing

from any of us, when our own
life-changing wars begin.

# Amnesia

Time tumbles downhill.
I examine the shadow
that used to be us,
try to remember
days when we felt passion,
when his love letters
filled my dresser drawer.

My lips are parched,
vagina sewn shut.
That part of me
has been excised,
a psychic lobotomy.
Have I died, a ghost
treading these rooms in parallel,
unseen, ignored?

The winds have come up.
They sound like the cry

of a thousand souls.
I think the dead cry with them

He rattles about in his Boston study,
war days supposedly over in our new life,
law books in his lap.
Soon we will sit at the table
in silence, arms bent.
Another day forgotten.
Another night yet to forget.

# Forgotten Places

In this new place
where birds fly upside
down, and sadness is a welt
made by a raindrop, he returns to me,
the scent of Hawaii upon him.

He speaks of sleep-talking dreamers,
whores dunked by blind preachers,
then kisses me like he once did.

I tug him inside
and we soar till our wings melt —
two candles, burnt to the nub
of a universe rebuilding.

We fall past old gods
converted to new ways of seeing
into the clear cleansing river of Eros
that finally Huck Finns us away.

## Measure of Time

Two months
three days into our marriage
and before his ship slipped dock
for its second Vietnam tour,
the first petal
dropped from the rose,
but was finally retrieved.

Five years
six months
three days later,
our apartment littered with petals
that could no longer be gathered,
I left.
Created a new life.
Cultivated, perhaps,
too many new gardens.

Twelve years,
six months,
two days
after our divorce was final,
I saw him in person for the last time.
We went to that old Indian dive
off Harvard Square.

Somewhere between
the hummus and rum balls,
we talked about our marriage.
Unresolved, like Vietnam.
Filled with regret, like Vietnam.
Too late to fix, like Vietnam,
but never forgotten,
like Vietnam.

## Parting

In my youth,
the Stones told me
time was on my side
and so I thought
our hours together
would stretch
over unseen horizons,
set anchor, hold fast.
That day as we divided
our old vinyls--
Joplin for me,
Butterfield for him,
mother's silver by my side,
and his father's clock on his,
I realized the Stones were wrong.
Our anchor had slipped,
dragging me backwards
across our wake
until the tide took me
and I drowned.

## Blood On the Wall

That war has visited
my thoughts often
in the years
since our men came home,
saturated with Agent Orange,
blood staining their hands,
hearts, and minds,
to fight yet another war
born from the rage of
our country turned
inside-out.

I think of the ones who
didn't return.
My throat closes.

The Wall.
Littered with names…
too many names.

Does their blood
weep from it at night,
seep into the grass?

A chance taken,
to touch home turf
one last time.

## Doing Time

Midnight. The whomp of a police 'copter.
I drift up from a dream, sink back,
ask the Dream Man if there's a support group
for Vietnam wives, marriages dead,
not their husbands.

But you appear, wearing those same dress whites
from our Pearl Harbor wedding,
new wife in red satin on your arm.
I forget the Dream Man, slink away,
Birkenstocks slapping the pavement
in my haste.

I thought you were lucky in your
supply ship assignment.
No jungle
No Napalm
One upriver
Shelled on that one time, a crew member lost
before the ship's escape.

I didn't see the war live on
in the wall you erected between us.

I was too young then to know that it takes
only one knife at the throat, one car wreck,
one rape to change a life and that the wall
you built was your prison, not mine.

# Truth and Other Lies

Huddled under Nam's deepening shadow
we drank too much wine,
ate burnt chicken, neglected
while wading the Hawaiian surf.

We strung shells into necklaces,
talismans for our husbands to take back to war,
promised friendships stretching to forever,
but it's been years now since we spoke.

I fall dizzily to ground
ear the tremor of grass blades,
hear old laughter and bare feet
sprinting across gray sand,
see youthful hands grasping for
futures never meant to be held tight.

## Cocoon

I still think of him when the spring
breezes blow floral and oceans roar,
my first love, who came back to Pearl
with Vietnam's angry heat
embedded into his pores,
not yet knowing he would rip out
the part of his heart
that once carried me in it so gently--
like a gestating baby, a safe cocoon
of dreams we didn't yet know would be
unraveled before the bootees were made.

# Who Sleeps With Him Now

Looking up from his book,
a half-smile traveled
from mouth to eyes.
I was thinking of us
in our eighties,
he said back then.

I have a recurring dream.
Us again, exiting that sparkle
of arched swords
into the blue Pearl Harbor air.

My current husband's tossing
awakens me.
I sit up.
Wonder.
Who sleeps with him now?

## Old bones

The white bones of our dreams
uncover, lie bare
when the tides are drawn back
by the Man in the Moon
His heart floated beneath mine
From my throat, his voice used to weep.
I was the surf
caressing his shore
the seas
lifting him high.
My wave rises, curls,
in its search,
but only old bones
tumble beyond my reach.

## My First Ex

He sent me her photo
when he finally remarried
at fifty, fifteen years
after our lingering cat and mouse,
after other attempts at romance
had ended.

She was round, like her glasses.
Not unpleasant, and a far safer bet
than I ever was with my
hippie hair, dangling earrings,
long legs stretching from mini's
like two show-offs.

Dr Phil would not
have recommended me.

He still emails me,
writes first about

his mother's death,
next, his father's, tells
me of deaths of friends
we had in common.
Flirts once, but I stop him.
Argues politics to rile me,
Sends photos of his adopted daughter,
later tells me of his cancer.

I remember loving him.
I remember when love
flew away, a giant swan
flapping itself free
from a once sparkling lake,
gradually transformed
into quicksand.

# Battlefield

His heart
is a battlefield
of scar tissue
and hardened walls
from radiation.
So certain a tumor
in his throat would take him
to his knees, wrench his life away
they brought forth
the beast... that fairy tale
of modern medicine
gone wrong.... and now
I want to call him,
tell him goodbye,
say it was good
part of the time
it lasted but his wife,
he tells his brother,
is uneasy with me

and so my first husband
will soon slip into the water
of time with no lei, no navy band
on Pearl Harbor's dock,
like when he came back
to me from Vietnam.

## Bed of Nails

No gypsy's tea leaves,
no crystal balls,
no voices in the night
warned me that he would lie
first on that bed of nails,
wings shorn,
pennies at the ready
for this day coming up faster
than a runaway train
towards that one day
which is to be his last.

He was my Anthony
before he hid behind his shield.
The thread between us
stretched, yet never quite broke.

I remember shining armor,
gardenias flavoring the breeze,

my bouquet pressed between
pages of a love story.

Now, with each breath a countdown,
I wonder if fire can once more
be swallowed into a man's belly.

## Untouched

My newly dead
ex-husband's letters
from Vietnam sit neatly
in a box in the chest
at bed's end.

I don't touch them.
I can't toss them.
I imagine him
in his ship's cabin
at night, my photo
pulled out, writing,
passing the time
between fuel pumps
to shore, imagining
our marriage, a baby...
(I especially don't read those).

When the ship got shelled
up-river after an oil line
broke he was shocked,
as if he had forgotten
the point of war was to kill,
but two more years after, when he
and his brother laughed
about 'gooks', live Cong tossed
from helicopters
like yesterday's trash,
the fraggings – the sort
of laughter that hides
a hole in the heart,
he assured me repeatedly
no, the war didn't affect
him at all.

## Over

Just when you think
the grieving is over,
when the rent
in the sky has sealed tight,
stars tumbled back into
position, the man in the moon
crawled out of hiding,
trees topple, houses crumble,
cars stall on abandoned roads.
He's gone to ash and won't come
back, no matter how many
times you pretend this was
just another bad dream
sent to torment you.

## Fourteen Months

from his ship in Vietnam.
Love letters.
Six pages in one of them
on the thin Navy stationary,
listing the ways he loved me.
Two months into his tour break
home with me at Pearl Harbor
I remember how I cramped his space.
I should have listened when
he said he stayed only because he promised.
Our apartment became webbed
with sadness
Butterflies flew from my chest,
fluttering out of his reach
into the fragrant Hawaii air.

Neither of us knew then that PTSD
could knock a man off-kilter
even on a relatively safe ship in the DMZ

He's dead two years and a half now,
both of us remarried,
but I still miss him.
Poems spill out
like the turning tide
he rode on then and ride
again now, touching me
occasionally within our shared
Vietnam of the soul.

## Contemplating My Mortality

I once imagined it would be him,
dancing between my thighs
during the days when I first
contemplated my mortality.

What else to think of a man
who brought me glass slippers,
and plaited my hair with sunlight
before spilling promises
as easily as cheap wine
in a brothel?

We declined into silence,
trapped among the cinders.
I mark off these charred days
with blood from my pricked finger.

Will I escape, I wondered;
flee to my pumpkin
before the clock strikes twelve?

Answers elude, but
when gravediggers appear
and women perfume my feet
with sage, should one soul
bend and softly inquire
about life's great
disappointment, I'll say,

you, dear,
it was you.

# Time's Tales

Grief is a place that digs deep holes
that can't be filled in with dirt or cement
or used clothes from Goodwill.
I open my chest to let a friend feel my grief
but it's his own grief he feels and he weeps.

He weeps for the young girls whose kisses
he missed, the friends who turned corners
and never came back, his lost sling shot
with his dad's initials carved on the handle.

He turns away, uncertain where he will go
to find himself now with loose ends dragging behind
like an albatross that won't let go.

I paint red over my wound for blood shed,
a reminder to honor the dead
as well another friend sitting beside me,
holding my hand, her own heart painted blue

to remind her of sunny days
that sit behind rain storms
even days when the rain never stops.

## For a Moment

I wake from a dream,
fingernails dug into his back,
his mouth hard on mine,
remembering those days that were
siphoned away and won't return
in this lifetime.
I was the one to leave,
so why the crocodile tears now?
One of his emails popped up
in an old folder yesterday
and, for a moment, I forgot he was dead,
doctors exhausted from attempts
at a heart restart and I want to answer
the email all over again just
like when I called mother's old number
until the line went silent,
telling her secrets I never
could utter when still alive.

# Flutter

A variegated green stone bird
dangles from a macrame cord
in some jewelry I'm going through.
Unseen in years.
A gift from my lost husband.

The dead one.

I hold it.
Memories flutter on its wings.
His love letters from Vietnam
and this lost/found bird
are all I have left of him.

His ashes drift.
Too late for looking back,
they whisper.

Too late to rerun back to the ship
dress-whiting into Pearl,
my name written on his heart,
arms reaching to greet;

too late to go back
to forevers that became never
before the story was done.

## Acknowledgments

Some poems have previously appeared as is or in a slightly different form in *The International War Veterans Poetry Archives (IWVPA)*, *Rusty Truck*, *Mipoeisa Journal (now Poets/Artists)*, *East to West*, *Pulse: the Voice of Medicine*, *Chiron Review*, *Shape of a Poem Anthology*, *The Dead Mule*, *Main Street Rag* and *In The Fray*. I want to thank all of these editors.

For their general encouragement and support, I thank Steve Clunk, my husband, friends Joe Zerbolio, Alan Peat, Margaret Walker, Alan Summers, Michael Rehling, Carole MacRury, the three poets who kindly wrote blurbs for my book ( and too many more writing friends to name ), members of the ME/CFS Living Your Plan group who help each other deal with the debilitating long term neuroimmune illness that has changed our lives, mine since 1990.

A special thanks to my wonderful publisher, Michael McInnis of Nixes Mate, who has always believed in me.

## About the author

The poems of Pris Campbell have appeared in numerous journals and anthologies, including *PoetsArtists*, *Nixes Mate*, *Rusty Truck*, *Bicycle Review*, *Chiron Review*, *Octopus Review*, *Boxcar Poetry Review*, and *Outlaw Poetry*. The Small Press has published eight collections of her poetry and Clemson University Press, a collaboration with Scott Owens. *My Southern Childhood*, from Nixes Mate is her most recent book. A former Clinical Psychologist, sailor and bicyclist until sidelined by ME/CFS in 1990, she makes her home with her current husband in the Greater West Palm Beach, Florida.

# 42° 19' 47.9" N  70° 56' 43.9" W

Nixes Mate is a navigational hazard in Boston Harbor used during the colonial period to gibbet and hang pirates and mutineers.

Nixes Mate Books features small-batch artisanal literature, created by writers who use all 26 letters of the alphabet and then some, honing their craft the time-honored way: one line at a time.

nixesmate.pub

www.ingramcontent.com/pod-product-compliance
Lightning Source LLC
Chambersburg PA
CBHW051808100526
44592CB00016B/2617